ANNE FRANK
THE DIARY OF A YOUNG GIRL

by
Anne Frank

Teacher Guide

Written by
Phyllis A. Green

Note

The Classic Pocket Book paperback edition of the book was used to prepare this guide. The page references may differ in the hardcover or other paperback editions.

Please note: Please assess the appropriateness of this play for the age level and maturity of your students prior to reading and discussing it with your class.

ISBN 1-56137-098-3

To order, contact your local school supply store, or—

Novel Units, Inc.
P.O. Box 791610
San Antonio, TX 78279

Web site: www.educyberstor.com

Table of Contents

Skills and Strategies

Thinking
Brainstorming, classifying
and categorizing, analyzing,
making generalizations,
drawing conclusions

Literary Elements
Character, setting, plot
development

Writing
Journal, narrative, poetry

Vocabulary
Context clues, prefixes,
suffixes and roots, key words

Comprehension
Predicting, sequencing,
cause/effect, inference

Listening/Speaking
Participation in discussion
groups

Summary of Anne Frank: The Diary of a Young Girl:
Anne Frank was a thirteen-year-old Jewish girl who lived in Holland during World War II. Because of the Nazi persecution of Jews during the German occupation of Holland, the Franks went into hiding. The book is Anne's diary written while living in the "Secret Annexe." The diary provides not only a historical account, but a warm poignant glimpse of Anne growing up, including her first adolescent love.

Initiating Activities:
1. Use the book as part of an integrated unit dealing with World War II. Specify the historical events from June 14, 1942, to August 1, 1944. As the diary is read, refer back to the historical events list. (See pages 26-28 of this guide.)

2. Brainstorm ideas about diaries.

3. For a week before starting the book, have students keep a diary/journal. Discuss feelings about journaling and what is expected of a journal style book.

4. Record what students know of the Holocaust and anti-Semitism in a list. After reading the book, revise the list to reflect what has been learned.

5. Look carefully at the picture of Anne Frank on the book's cover. What predictions can you make of this author?

6. Stage a multi-media visit to the time period of the book. Play music of the early forties. List events of the time period. Invite speakers to the classroom.

7. Simulation of Discrimination: Distribute cards to all students or number off. Then announce that certain numbers or cards won't go to recess or get some treat. Then announce that those people must move their desks to a corner. Discuss how discrimination makes you feel.

Vocabulary Activities: (See reproducible vocabulary challenge "cards" on pages 22-25 of this guide.)

1. Semantic Feature Analysis: Prepare a chart to analyze words. a) Choose a category; b) List several examples of the category in the left hand column. Across the top list possible descripters with a plus or minus.

Category-Fruit	Eat Raw	Seeds	Have Peelings	Red
Apple	+ -	+	+	+ -
Pear	+	+	+	-
Peach	+ -	+	+	-
Banana	+	-	+	-

2. Divide the class into pairs or groups to figure out ways for classmates to remember assigned words or groups of words. Mnemonic devices, pantomimes, or other tricks are encouraged. Teach your words to classmates.

3. Especially for adjectives, make up fragments to be completed.

Irate: angry

My mother was so irate that she _____.

My mother was irate when _____.

4. Look for the vocabulary words in the story. Use context clues. Context strategies include:

    a) Looking for what part of speech the word is.
    b) Use synonyms or appositives.
    c) Contrast.
    d) Author describes the word directly.
    e) Cause-effect.

5. Learn about prefixes, suffixes, and roots of English words. Introduce some prefixes, suffixes, and roots to the class. Let class members add other examples.

> ante: before
> anti: against
> contra: against
> hemi: half
> poly: many
> pre: before
> syn: with, together
> uni: one

6. Speed Dictionary: Post vocabulary challenge words. Students look up definitions in dictionaries, striving for speed. Team play is a possible adaptation.

7. Complete a word map for some of the vocabulary challenge words. The word map is best used with nouns, but can be adapted for other parts of speech.

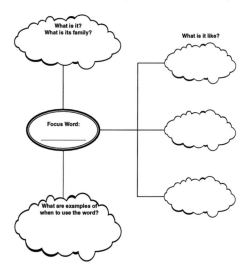

8. Students define words, then play twenty questions giving characteristics for classmates to guess the word. For example, vegetable soup (served for lunch, with crackers, hot, served in a bowl, mostly liquid, food).

9. Record new words on 3 x 5 cards to study at odd moments. Record definitions on one side and sentence where word occurred on the other. Use as flashcards.

Using Predictions in the Novel Unit Approach

We all make predictions as we read—little guesses about what will happen next, how the conflict will be resolved, which details given by the author will be important to the plot, which details will help to fill in our sense of a character. Students should be encouraged to predict, to make sensible guesses. As students work on predictions, these discussion questions can be used to guide them: What are some of the ways to predict? What is the process of a sophisticated reader's thinking and predicting? What clues does an author give us to help us in making our predictions? Why are some predictions more likely than others?

A predicting chart is for students to record their predictions. As each subsequent chapter is discussed, you can review and correct previous predictions. This procedure serves to focus on predictions and to review the stories.

Use the facts and ideas the author gives.

Use your own knowledge.

Use new information that may cause you to change your mind.

Predictions:

_____

_____

_____

_____

Prediction Chart

What characters have we met so far?	What is the conflict in the story?	What are your predictions?	Why did you make those predictions?

Introductory Notes, Preface, Introduction

Vocabulary:

poignantly ix

Discussion Questions and Activities:

1. When was the book first published? *(1947)*

2. What was the original title of the book? *(Het Achterhuis, the house behind)*

3. What does George Stevens include in the Preface and Introduction to the book? *(He emphasizes Anne's will for survival and explains how the diary survived. The Green Police who discovered the hiding place discarded the papers in Mr. Frank's brief case, loaded up the silverware and Hanukkah candlestick and led the group away.)*

4. What does Eleanor Roosevelt feel of the book? *(She considers it a remarkable book and a testimony to the spirit of Anne Frank.)* Who was Eleanor Roosevelt? *(Franklin Delano Roosevelt's wife and U.S. first lady from 1933-1945.)*

5. What is the significance of Anne Frank's note at the start of the diary? *(Candor expected in the entries; Anne felt alone as she wrote.)*

Sunday, 14 June, 1942 to Tuesday, 22 December, 1942— Pages 1-56

Vocabulary:

unbosomings 2	pogroms 3	speculation 5	superfluous 11
obstinate 24	surreptitiously 27	seclusion 32	quicksilver 33
Gestapo 34	rendezvous 45	lorries 48	camomile 53

Discussion Questions and Activities:

1. What is significant about June 14, 1942, the book's first entry? *(Anne's birthday)*

2. Who is Kitty? *(Anne's name for her diary; Anne addresses all her diary entries to Kitty.)*

3. What was Anne's life like before entering the "Secret Annexe"? *(She had many friends, attended Jewish Secondary School, and was a high-spirited adolescent. Her family appears well-to-do, but there are anti-Jewish laws being enacted.)*

4. Who are Zionists? *(Jewish people who support re-establishing a Jewish state in Palestine.)*

5. What has turned Anne's whole world upside down in her July 8, 1942 report? *(A call-up notice has been sent for Margot, Anne's sister, and the family decided to go into hiding.)*

6. How were Jews treated in 1942 Holland? *(There were anti-Jewish laws, and they had to wear yellow Stars of David.)*

7. Who lives in the "Secret Annexe"? *(the Franks, the Van Daans, and Mr. Dussel)* How do these people get along with each other? *(varied reactions, including normal human disagreements and bickering)*

8. What are some of the adaptations the "Secret Annexe" residents have to make in hiding? *(quiet all the time, washing only on Sundays)*

9. How does Anne spend her time in the "Secret Annexe"? *(reading, learning shorthand, doing lessons with father, eating, listening to radio, talking)*

10. How does Anne resemble most thirteen-year-olds you know? *(Answers vary. She has middle school adolescent ways—ups and downs. She tries to make sense of the adult world. She is beginning to notice boys and to note male-female relationships.)*

Supplementary Activities:
1. Writing: If you were going into hiding, what would you take with you? Why?

2. Thinking and Writing: The Franks decide to go into hiding in Holland rather than try to escape to another country. Why do you think they made that choice? What would be your choice?

3. Bulletin Board: Prepare a charting of the rooms in the "Secret Annexe" to help visualize what Anne is writing about. (See page 16 of the book.)

4. Writing: While reading the book, keep a journal. Write daily about whatever is happening in your life.

Wednesday, 13 January, 1943 to Tuesday, 13 July, 1943— Pages 57-79

Vocabulary:

venom 59	discord 59	procured 61	haricot beans 63
eucalyptus 67	duodenal ulcer 75	clandestine 75	barrage 77
het 78	pedantic 79		

Discussion Questions and Activities:

1. Why does Anne think she is fortunate compared to others? *(She is safe and quiet. Others have to beg for a piece of bread.)*

2. Why do you think Anne writes so often about arguments? *(It is hard to live as the Franks are living—very close to other people. Not being able to go elsewhere probably causes Anne and her family to dwell on family squabbles.)*

3. Anne uses a lot of synonyms for arguments. What are some of these synonyms? Try to extend the chain:

   row—discord—atmosphere is strained—boiling with rage—fuss—quarrels

4. How does Anne spend her days? Compare her typical activities to your typical activities.

Anne	You
•*Reading* •*Foreign words on cards* •*Shorthand* •*Studying* •*Listening to the radio*	

5. How do the "Secret Annexe" folk hide their existence? *(They try to conceal clues to the increased people in the building—garbage, noise, water, and electric usage.)*

6. What does Pim's birthday poem for Anne tell you of their relationship? *(Pim understands about the difficulties and strains for Anne. He applauds her efforts and loves her.)*

Supplementary Activities:

1. Writing: Choose one of your journal entries to edit and polish into a finished essay to share with classmates.

2. Complete a sociogram to explore Anne's relationships with the other characters. (See page 9 of this guide.)

3. Look back to the floor plan of the "Secret Annexe" on page 16. Estimate the square footage of the area. Mark off in your classroom. Assign eight students to sit in the space. How does it make you feel?

Sociogram

Directions: On the lines, use one word to describe the relationship between the characters. Remember that relationships go both ways and that each line needs a descriptive word.

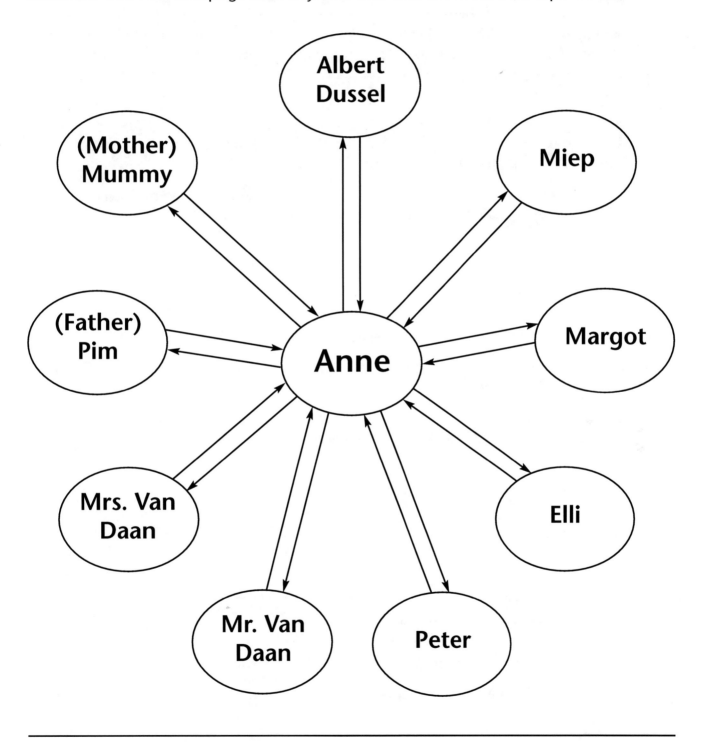

Friday, 16 July, 1943 to Wednesday, 29 December, 1943— Pages 80-114

Vocabulary:

tumult 81	dispersed 82	coquetry 84	supple 85
eiderdown 86	irrevocable 90	incessantly 93	capitulated 97
grouses 100	palpitations 103	consolation 105	cremated 105
lozenges 109	compresses 109		

Discussion Questions and Activities:

1. How are those in the "Secret Annexe" able to survive? Where do they get food? Who helps them? *(Mr. Frank's former employers and friends secretly bring them food, books, and whatever they need.)*

2. What would happen to those in hiding if they got sick and required medical care? How do those in hiding deal with sickness? *(home remedies and what medicine friends provide)*

3. What are the first wishes of those in the "Secret Annexe" when they are able to leave? *(to have a hot bath filled to overflowing, seeing his wife, eat cream cakes, see a cinema, visit friends)* What would your first wish be if you were in such a situation?

4. What deficiencies does Anne see in Mrs. Van Daan? *(page 84, Thursday, 29 July, 1943)*

5. Explain 24 hours in the "Secret Annexe." *(pages 86-91, Wednesday, 4 August, 1943-Monday, 9 August, 1943)*

6. Draw the dinner table at the "Secret Annexe" with an adjective for each diner. *(pages 90-91; some suggested adjective answers below)*

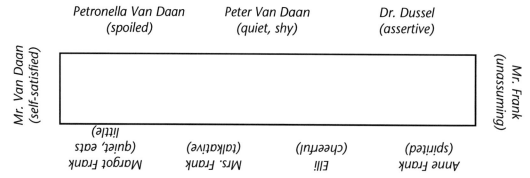

7. Dramatize potato peeling. *(page 93, Wednesday, 18 August, 1943)*

8. Why would a fountain pen be a special friend to someone like Anne?

Supplementary Activities:
1. This book is a translation from the Dutch. What are the special challenges of a translation? Invite to the class someone whose first language isn't English. Discuss translating.

2. Create a word map representing the challenges of living in the "Secret Annexe." Include internal and external concerns as well as survival needs.

3. Reread Anne's "Ode to My Fountain Pen" on pages 104-105. Write an ode to a favorite tool of yours. (pen, computer, recorder, paints, etc.)

Sunday, 2 January, 1944 to Friday, 31 March, 1944— Pages 114-174

Vocabulary:

aggravating 115	fortnight 122	diligently 122	suffice 124
sauntered 128	genealogical 129	impudent 132	rummaging 137
scoffingly 150	coquettish 151	kale 156	hemorrhage 158
incessantly 159	sallies 167	stupendous 169	

Discussion Questions and Activities:
1. In her January 22, 1944 entry, Anne asks why people always try to hide their real feelings. What are some possible answers? Choose one of your answers and write a short paragraph to explain the answer. You could use examples from the book in your paragraph.

2. Anne thinks Peter has an inferiority complex. Find examples in the diary to support that idea. *(He is quiet, shy. Although he is Jewish, he thinks it would be easier to be Christian.)*

3. On February 23, 1944, Anne includes a thought about what is missed by being in hiding and how they must find inward compensation. What are some of the things Anne and the others miss while in hiding? *(freedom, independence; gardens, nature; solitude—chance to be alone; many friends, interaction with lots of other people; choices; varied entertainments)*

4. Why do you think Anne writes more and more of Peter Van Daan? *(She is an adolescent and he seems to be her "first love." He is the only young man in the "Secret Annexe.")*

5. Who are the people who support those in hiding? What is the Underground, the Resistance? Why do these people take on the work?

6. How do Anne and Margot work out their "competition" over Peter Van Daan? *(by writing letters)* What do you discover about the relationship between the sisters from the letters? *(They really do care for each other's feelings.)* What other ways have you seen siblings settle concerns? Write a short paragraph to describe one such instance.

7. What do you know of Anne from her diary? Record your answers on an attribute web. (See graphic below and pages 15-17 of this guide.)

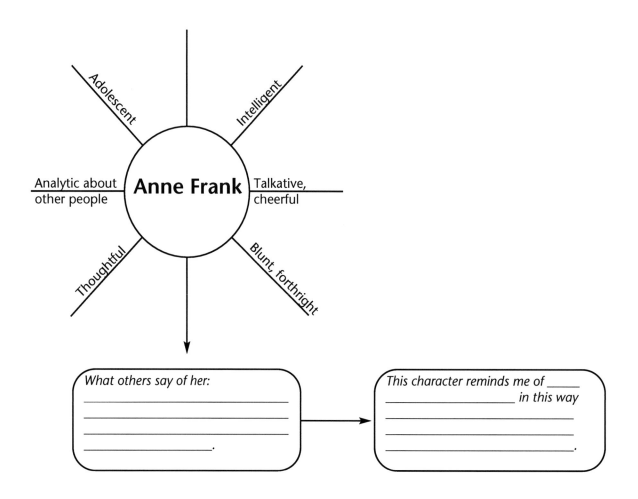

8. Anne seems to have differences with her mother. Why? Find some examples in the book to support your explanation.

14

Using Character Webs—In the Novel Unit Approach

Attribute Webs are simply a visual representation of a character from the novel. They provide a systematic way for the students to organize and recap the information they have about a particular character. Attribute webs may be used after reading the novel to recapitulate information about a particular character or completed gradually as information unfolds, done individually, or finished as a group project.

One type of character attribute web uses these divisions:

● How a character acts and feels. (How does the character feel in this picture? How would you feel if this happened to you? How do you think the character feels?)

● How a character looks. (Close your eyes and picture the character. Describe him to me.)

● Where a character lives. (Where and when does the character live?)

● How others feel about the character. (How does another specific character feel about our character?)

In group discussion about the student attribute webs and specific characters, the teacher can ask for backup proof from the novel. You can also include inferential thinking.

Attribute webs need not be confined to characters. They may also be used to organize information about a concept, object or place.

Attribute Web

The attribute web below is designed to help you gather clues the author provides about what a character is like. Fill in the blanks with words and phrases which tell how the character acts and looks, as well as what the character says and what others say about him or her.

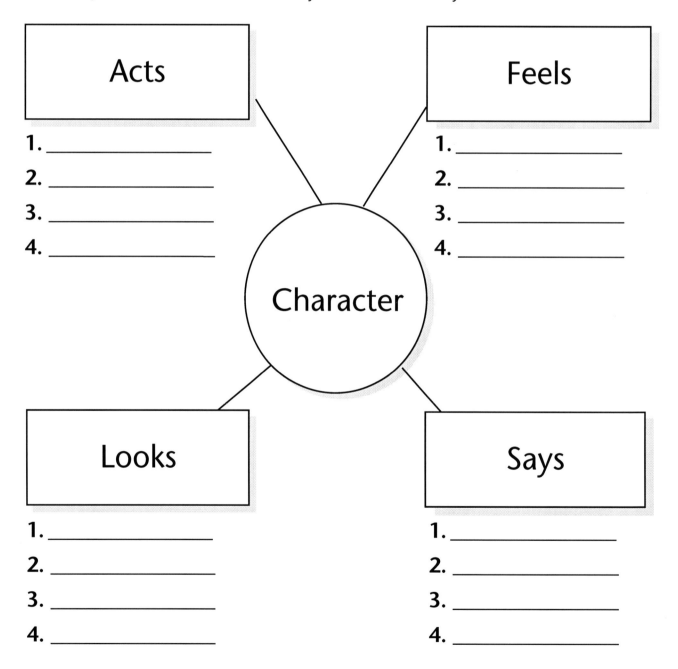

Attribute Web

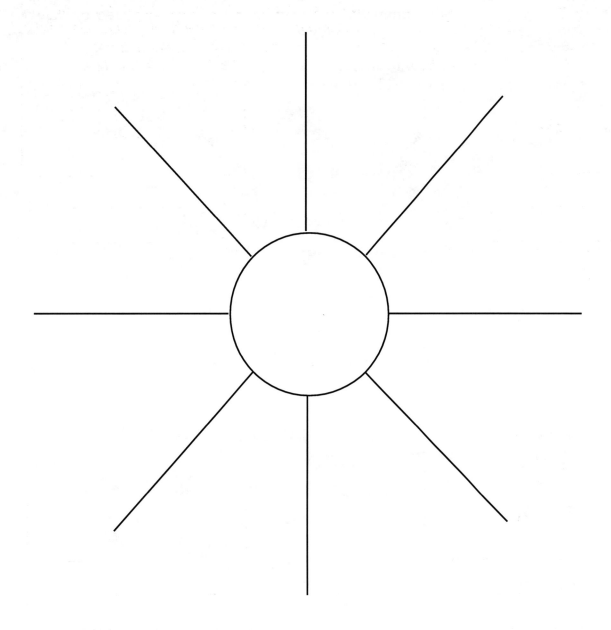

Supplementary Activities:
1. Using a calendar of the book's time period, plot Anne's moods. You may use facial illustrations or one-word summaries. Why is it important that characters be shown with ups and downs and varied moods?

2. What is special about a confidante and friend? Why is this such a need for Anne? With a classmate complete a web of your ideas.

3. What kind of music, art, and books of today would Anne Frank like? Defend your choices using information from the book.

Saturday, 1 April, 1944 to Sunday Morning, 7 May, 1944— Pages 174-205

Vocabulary:

endive 175	kohlrabi 175	beetroot 176	impudence 180
reproached 186	livid 189	pseudonym 193	jocular 196
piccalilli 200	clandestine 204		

Discussion Questions and Activities:
1. What are the food cycles Anne describes on April 3, 1944? *(periods when one has nothing else to eat but one particular dish or kind of vegetable)* Can you think of any "food cycles" in your life? *(turkey at Thanksgiving, sweet corn, strawberries, zucchini)* Choose a food cycle to describe, including your feelings eating at that time.

2. What are Anne's hobbies? *(page 178)* Why does she have so many hobbies? *(She has many interests and enthusiasms and hasn't concentrated on one hobby yet.)*

3. In Anne's April 11, 1944 entry, she tells of a warehouse break-in and then asks some philosophical questions about Jews. Discuss these questions with your classmates. Do you agree with Anne's explanation written in 1944? Would her answer be different today?

4. How have Anne's entries in the diary changed in April, 1944? *(more questions)*

5. What is Anne's major run-in with her father in April, 1944? *(After he asks her to stop going upstairs to talk to Peter every evening, Anne's father receives a letter from Anne setting forth her complaints about her treatment while in hiding. Pim tells her that her parents do not deserve such a reproach. They do talk it out and Anne is forgiven.)*

Supplementary Activities:
1. Share Anne's entries of May 5, 6, and 7, 1944 with a parent. Ask for their reactions.

2. Compute in dollars and cents the cost of various items described on May 6, 1944. Remember that these are 1944 prices. Why are they so high?

3. Investigate the organization and status of occupied Netherlands during World War II.

4. What advice would you give Anne and her parents?

Monday, 8 May, 1944 to Tuesday, 1 August, 1944—Pages 205-241

Vocabulary:

teetotaler 206	concentration camps 209	coherent 209	capping 211
incalculable 213	loathed 213	explicitly 214	asylum 215
discord 215	abyss 216	dregs 216	capitulation 219
redoubt 223	scudding 226	supercilious 241	

Discussion Questions and Activities:
1. Anne says, "The world is a queer place!" *(page 207)* She is referring to her circumstances compared to her grandparents. Explain. *(Both her father's and her mother's families were rich and now Margot and Anne are in hiding with hardly enough to eat.)*

2. What is Anne's career ambition? *(to be a journalist and famous writer)* Is it an appropriate ambition? Why?

3. On May 26, 1944, Anne wonders about whether they should have gone into hiding. Why do you think she voices such a thought?

4. Why is the Allied invasion (D-Day) a cause for rejoicing? *(It is the start of liberation of the occupied countries and defeat of the Germans.)*

5. On Anne's fifteenth birthday, she makes an accounting of her plusses and minuses. Fill in a chart for her as the various friends would do.

Plus	Minus
Peter: Affectionate Pim: Intelligent Elli: Fun	Mrs. Van Daan: Stupid Pim: Unappreciative to parents

6. How do the "Secret Annexers" deal with 26 trays of strawberries? *(jam, eat strawberries with porridge, skimmed milk, for dessert, with sugar)*

Supplementary Activities:
1. Identify these terms from the book: Whitsun, D-Day, Churchill, Smuts, Eisenhower, Arnold, Mussert.

2. On page 227 (Friday, 16 June, 1944), Anne states her golden rule. What is it? What other golden rules do you know? Make a list and add some new ideas of your own. Share with a classmate and continue to expand your lists.

3. Discuss the strawberry abundance with someone who "cans." What is the process?

Epilogue and Afterword—Pages 242-258

Vocabulary:

indignation 245	totalitarian 247	foreboding 248	acquiesced 248
appeasement 249	deportation 252	crematories 254	emaciated 255

Discussion Questions and Activities:
1. What happened to the "Secret Annexe" on August 4, 1944? *(The inhabitants plus Kraler and Koophuis were arrested and sent to German and Dutch concentration camps.)*

2. Why do we have Anne's diary today? *(Miep and Elli found it after the others were arrested. The diary was translated into English.)*

3. What was the fate of those imprisoned? *(only Anne's father and Kraler and Koophuis survived. Anne died in March, 1945.)*

Summarizing Activities

1. Make a list of some questions you'd ask if you could interview Anne Frank. Trade questions with classmates who will devise answers.

2. Why should this book be required reading before graduating from high school?

3. What is Anne Frank's philosophy of life? What ideas of hers are applicable as much today as in 1944?

4. Show the movie made from the book. (available from Novel Units) How are the two similar? What are some distinctions arising from the particular medium—print, cinema?

5. If Anne had lived, what would she be doing today? Prepare a scenario of her life.

6. What shocked you most in the book? Why?

7. Using the summarizing spinner below, each student (or small group) takes a turn to spin and answer.

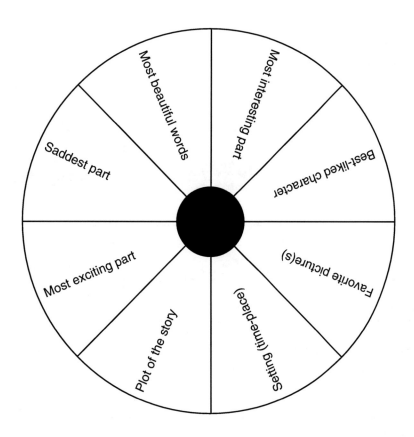

Vocabulary Words

poignantly	unbosomings	pogroms
speculation	superfluous	obstinate
surreptitiously	seclusion	quicksilver
Gestapo	rendezvous	lorries
camomile	venom	discord
procured	haricot beans	eucalyptus
duodenal ulcer	clandestine	barrage
het	pedantic	tumult

dispersed	coquetry	supple
eiderdown	irrevocable	incessantly
capitulated	grouses	palpitations
consolation	cremated	lozenges
compresses	aggravating	fortnight
diligently	suffice	sauntered
genealogical	impudent	rummaging
scoffingly	coquettish	kale

hemorrhage	incessantly	sallies
stupendous	endive	kohlrabi
beetroot	impudence	reproached
livid	pseudonym	jocular
piccalilli	clandestine	teetotaler
concentration camps	coherent	capping
incalculable	loathed	explicitly
asylum	discord	abyss

dregs	capitulation	redoubt
scudding	supercilious	indignation
totalitarian	foreboding	acquiesced
appeasement	deportation	crematories
emaciated		

Teacher Information

Holocaust: The mass murder of European Jews by the Nazis during World War II. About six million Jewish men, women, and children (about 2/3 of the Jews in Europe) were exterminated in Nazi dictator Adolf Hitler's plan to wipe out the entire Jewish population. Other ethnic groups killed were Gypsies, Poles, and Slavs. On the night of November 9, 1938, Kristallnacht, the night of broken glass, dozens of Jews were killed, between 20,000 and 30,000 Jews were sent to concentration camps, more than 200 synagogues were burned or demolished, and 7,500 Jewish-owned businesses were destroyed. That night marked the start of the intense persecution. The concentration camps where the Jews were imprisoned were horrible places with gas chambers where many Jews were exterminated and others starved or died of disease.

World War II (1939-1945) killed more people and brought more destruction than any other war in history. At the conclusion, western Europe as the center of world power had fallen. The war began on September 1, 1939, when Germany invaded Poland. Germany's dictator, Adolf Hitler, directed his powerful war machine to defeat and occupy Poland, Denmark, Luxembourg, the Netherlands, Belgium, Norway, and France. By June, 1940, Great Britain stood alone against Hitler. Italy, under Mussolini, joined the war on Germany's side (the Axis) in June, 1940. Fighting spread to Greece and north Africa and the Soviet Union. The Japanese attack on Pearl Harbor in Hawaii brought the United States into the war in December, 1941. The Allies (United States, Great Britain, China, and the Soviet Union) fought against the Axis Powers (Germany, Italy, and Japan). The war concluded with an Allied victory, Germany surrendering on May 7, 1945, and Japan surrendering on September 2, 1945.

Important Dates in the War:

1939

September 1:	Germany invaded Poland.
September 3:	Britain and France declared war on Germany.

1940

April 9:	Germany invaded Denmark and Norway.
May 10:	Germany invaded Belgium and the Netherlands.
June 10:	Italy entered the war on the German side.
June 22:	France signed an armistice with Germany.
July 10:	Battle of Britain (an air campaign by Germany to defeat Britain's Royal Air Force)

1941

April 6:	Germany invaded Greece and Yugoslavia.
June 22:	Germany invaded the Soviet Union.
September 8:	Germany blockaded Leningrad.
December 7:	Japan bombed United States base at Pearl Harbor.
December 8:	United States, Britain, and Canada declared war on Japan.

1942

February 15:	Singapore fell to Japanese.
February 26-28:	Japan defeated Allied forces in Battle of the Java Sea.
April 9:	United States and Philippine troops surrendered on Bataan Peninsula.
April 18:	United States bombers hit Tokyo.
May 4-8:	Allies checked Japanese assault in Battle of the Coral Sea.
June 4-6:	Allies defeated Japan in the Battle of Midway.
August 7:	United States marines landed in Guadalcanal.
August 25:	Hitler ordered his troops to capture Stalingrad.
October 23:	Britain attacked the Axis in Egypt.
November 8:	Allied troops landed in Algeria and Morocco.

1943

February 2:	The last Germans surrendered at Stalingrad.
May 13:	Axis forces in Africa surrendered.
July 4:	Germany opened assault on Kursk.
July 10:	Allied forces invaded Sicily.
September 3:	Italy surrendered to the Allies.

September 9:	Allied troops landed at Salerno, Italy.
November 20:	United States forces invaded Tarawa.

1944

June 6:	D-Day (Allied invasion on Normandy Beach)
June 19-20:	United States naval force defeated Japanese in Battle of the Philippine Sea.
July 18:	Japan's prime minister resigned.
July 20:	Plot to assassinate Hitler failed.
October 20:	Allies began landing in the Philippines.
October 23-26:	Allies defeated Japan's navy in the Battle of Leyte Gulf in the Philippines.
December 16:	Battle of the Bulge (German surprise attack in the Ardennes Forest in Belgium and Luxembourg)

1945

March 16:	United States marines captured Iwo Jima.
April 30:	Hitler took his life in Berlin.
May 7:	Germany's unconditional surrender.
June 21:	Allied forces captured Okinawa.
August 6:	Atomic bomb dropped on Hiroshima.
August 8:	Atomic bomb dropped on Nagasaki.
August 14:	Japan's unconditional surrender.
September 2:	Japan signed surrender terms.

© Novel Units, Inc.

28

Selected Bibliography of Related Literature:

Adler, David A. *We Remember the Holocaust.* New York: H. Holt, 1989. Summary: Discusses the events of the Holocaust and includes personal accounts from survivors of their experiences of the persecution and the death camps.

Bergman, Tamar. *Along the Tracks.* (Translated from the Hebrew by Michael Swirsky.) Boston: Houghton Mifflin, 1991. Summary: Recounts the adventures of a young Jewish boy who is driven from his home by the German invasion, becomes a refugee in the Soviet Union, is separated from his family, and undergoes many hardships before enjoying a normal home again.

Bishop, Claire Huchet. *Twenty and Ten.* New York: Puffin Books, 1978, 1952. Summary: Twenty school children hide ten Jewish children from the Nazis occupying France during World War II.

Forman, James D. *The Survivor.* New York: Farrar, Straus & Giroux, 1976. Summary: An account of a Jewish family in Holland during World War II as one by one it dwindles away during the Nazi Holocaust.

Herman, Erwin. *The Yanov Torah.* Rockville, MD: Kar-Ben Copies, 1985. Summary: Jews in a work camp in Yanov during the Nazi occupation of L'vov, Poland, smuggle in a Torah, piece by piece, despite enormous personal danger.

Isaacman, Clara. *Clara's Story.* Philadelphia: Jewish Publication Society of America, 1984. Summary: The author describes her own and her family's experiences during the two and one-half years they spent in hiding in Antwerp, Belgium, during World War II.

Mace, Elisabeth. *Brother Enemy.* New York: Beaufort Books, 1979. Summary: Sent from Nazi Germany to England to spend the war years with his Jewish father, Andreas continues to yearn for his home and make plans for his return.

Rossel, Seymour. *The Holocaust.* New York: Watts, 1981. Summary: Discusses how, between 1938 and 1945, the Nazis planned and carried out a program of extermination against the Jews of Europe now known as the Holocaust, and how the Holocaust continues to affect our everyday lives.

Schnabel, Ernst. *Anne Frank: A Portrait in Courage.* New York: Harcourt, Brace, 1958.

Stein, R. Conrad. *Warsaw Ghetto.* Chicago: Children's Press, 1985. Summary: Recounts life in the Jewish quarter in Warsaw from 1939 to 1945 when the years of hunger and privation culminated in the complete destruction of that ghetto.

Suhl, Yuri. *On the Other Side of the Gate, a Novel*. New York: F. Watts, 1975. Summary: Relates to experiences of a young Jewish couple when they are confined to a ghetto during the German occupation of Poland in World War II.

Treseder, Terry W. *Hear O Israel: A Story of the Warsaw Ghetto*. New York: Atheneum, 1990. Summary: A Jewish boy describes life in the Warsaw ghetto and his family's ultimate transference to and decimation in the camp of Treblinka.

Zeinert, Karen. *The Warsaw Ghetto Uprising*. Brookfield, CT: Millbrook Press, 1993. Summary: Describes life in the section of Warsaw where Polish Jews were confined by the Nazis and discusses the activities of the Jewish resistance prior to the destruction of the ghetto in 1943.

Story Map

```
   ⬭ Setting ⬭
        │
        ▼
   ⬭ Problem ⬭
        │
        ▼
   ⬭  Goal  ⬭
        │
        ▼
  ⬭ Episodes ⬭
        │
        ▼
 ⬭ Resolution ⬭
```

Characters_____

_____

_____

_____

Time and Place_____

_____

_____

_____

_____

Beginning ⟶ Development ⟶ Outcome

_____

_____

_____

_____

_____

_____

_____

_____

Assessment for *Anne Frank: The Diary of a Young Girl*

Assessment is an on-going process, more than a quiz at the end of the book. Points may be added to show the level of achievement. When an item is completed, the teacher and the student check it.

Name _____ Date _____

Student   **Teacher**

_____   _____   1. Make your own type of story map for the novel. (See page 31 of this guide.)

_____   _____   2. Writing: If you were going into hiding, what would you take with you? Why?

_____   _____   3. Research the organization and status of occupied Netherlands during World War II.

_____   _____   4. With a classmate take turns retelling one of the episodes from the point of view of someone other than Anne.

_____   _____   5. Divide a sheet of paper in four sections. What are the four most important parts of this story? Draw an illustration for each of these important parts.

_____   _____   6. Make an attribute web for Peter. (See pages 15-17 of this guide.)

_____   _____   7. Complete at least six vocabulary activities. (See pages 4-5 of this guide.)

_____   _____   8. Create a mobile based on the story.

_____   _____   9. Change two things in this novel and explain how the changes would make a difference. Make a list of these changes and compare with a classmate's list.

_____   _____   10. Write a ten question quiz for a classmate. Make an answer sheet.